A a
is for Anansi

Spider

A a
is for Ackee

Jamaica's National fruit; cooked with saltfish becomes Jamaica's national dish

B b
is for Batty jaw

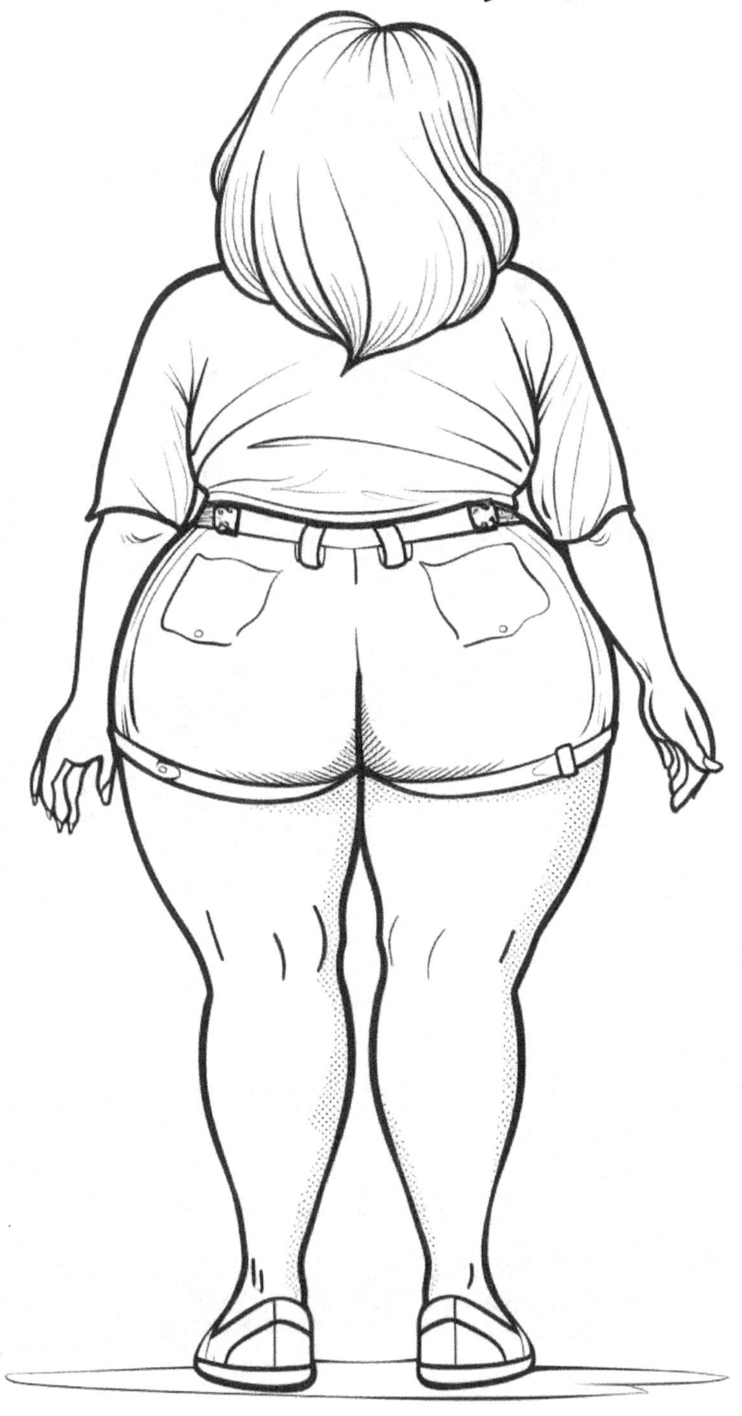

Lower part of the buttock

B b
is for Bang belly

A protruding waistline

B b
is for Batty bwoy

A gay/ homosexual male

B b
is for breakfront

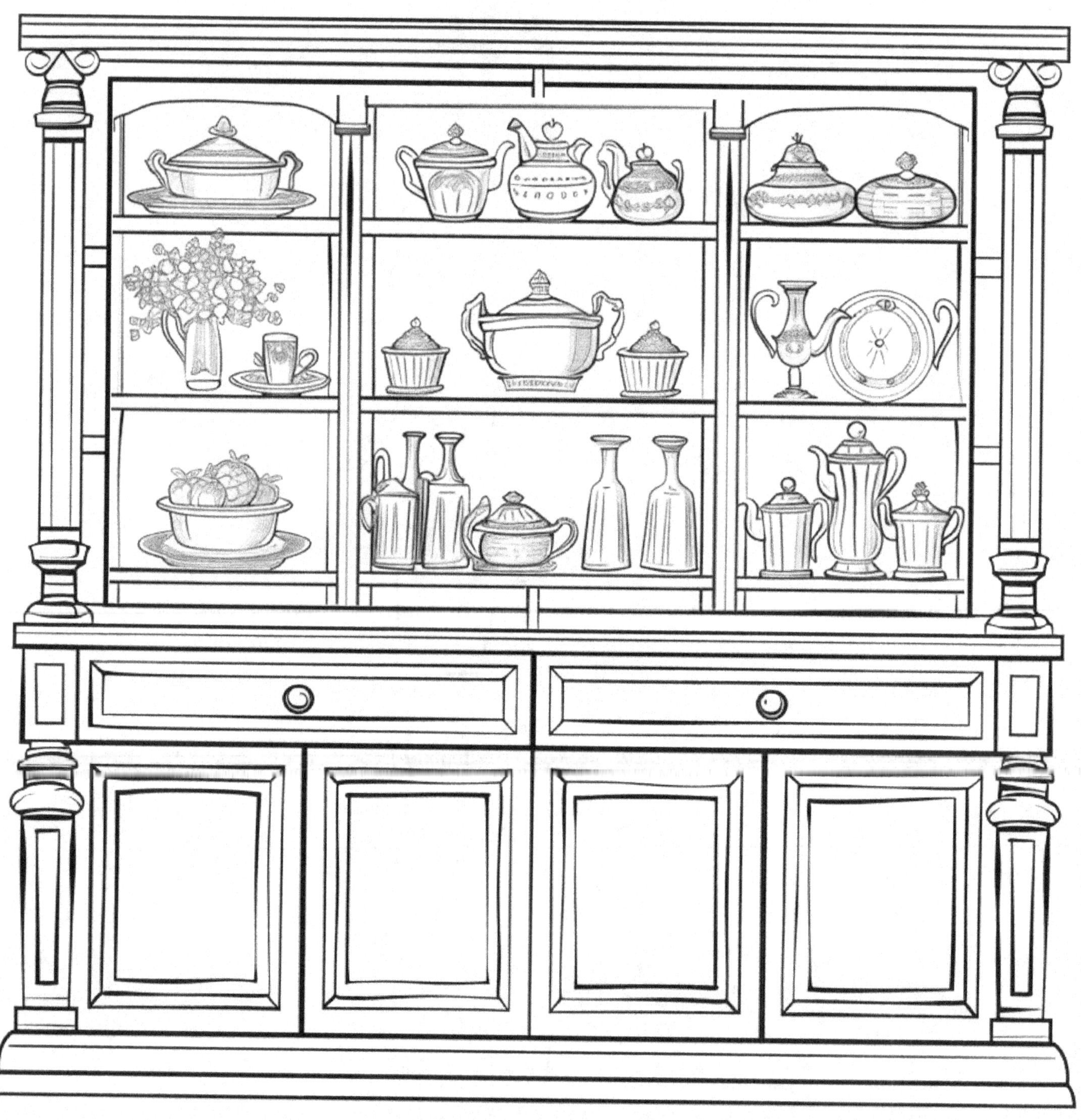

Piece of wooden furniture that stored the family matriarch's
most prized stoneware and cutlery

C c
is for Coolie

A person of indian descent

C c
is for Choppa

A person known for lottery scamming activity

C c
is for Coal Pot

A small wood burning stove

D d
is for Dread

A Rastafarian male

D d
is for Drankro

A vulture; a despicable person

D d
is for drops

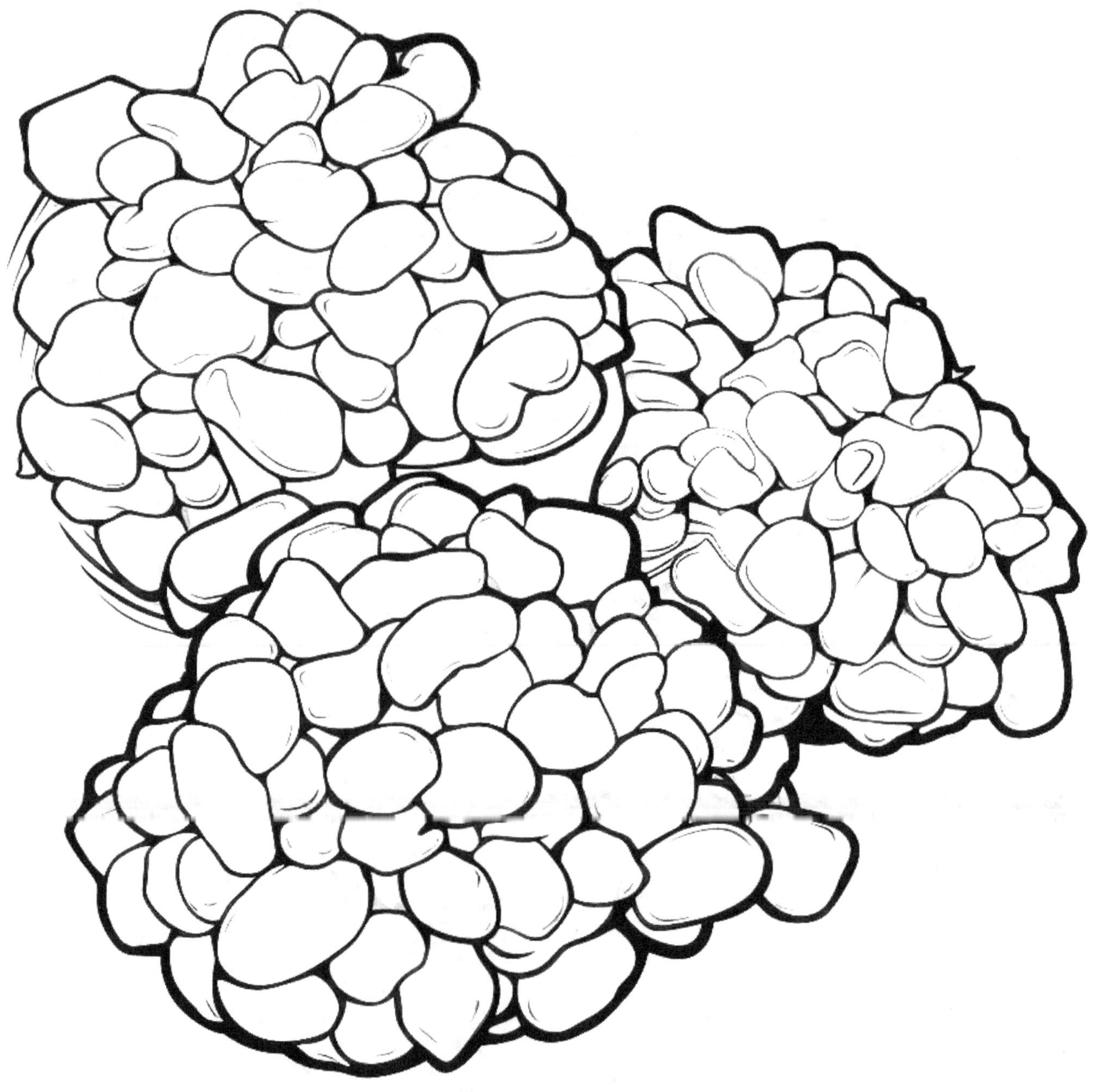

A sweet treat made from diced coconut cooked in cane sugar
with ginger and spices and allowed to harden

E e
is for Enamel Mug

An enamel mug usually for having organic hot cocoa

F f
is for Fab

Powdered detergent

F f
is for Flaw-flaw

Homemade pastries, mainly cakes and puddings

G g
is for Goat kid

A baby goat

G g
is for Gizzada

A pastry made of shredded coconut, cooked and reduced in sugar,
baked in a crunchy round crust with pinched edges

G g
is for Game cock

A rooster used mainly for illegal animal fighting

H h
is for Hummin' bird

Our national bird, the Doctor bird, is a humming bird

I i
is for Ignarant

Describes a person who is easily angered

J j
is for Jackass

A donkey

J j
is for jinja

Ginger root

K k
is for kakafaat

An expression of shock

L l

is for Lignum vitae

Jamaica's national flower

L l

is for Louns

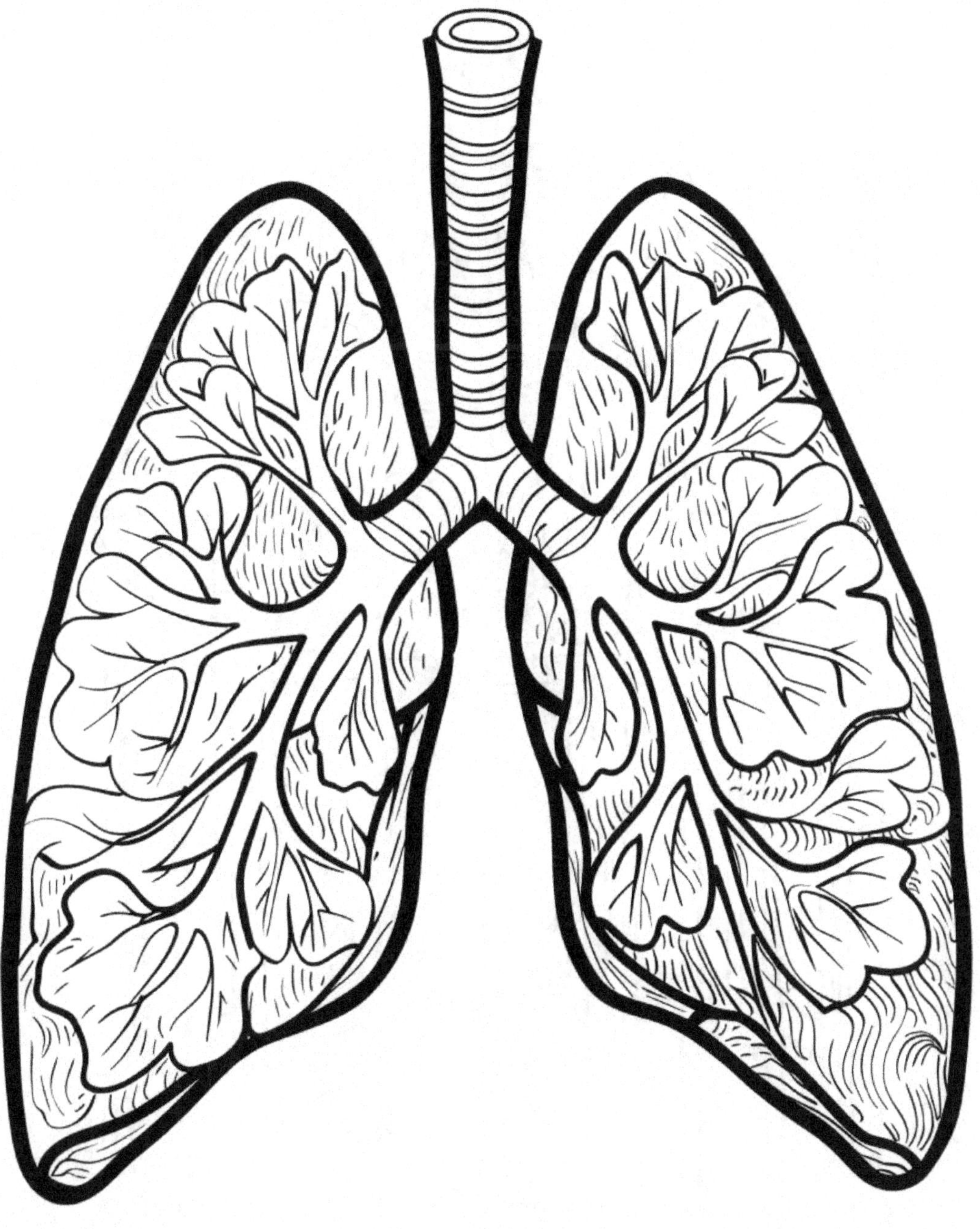

The lungs

M m
is for Muss-muss

A small mouse

M m
is for Mongrel

A dog of mixed breed

M m
is for Mampy

A plus-sized woman

N n
is for Nanny

Our only national heroine

N n
is for Nose-hole

Nostrils

O o
is for Obeah wucka

A practitioner of witchcraft

O o
is for Overlook

The act of observing a baby lovingly

O o
is for Ole bruk

Used items, mainly clothing and shoes

P p
is for Pumpum

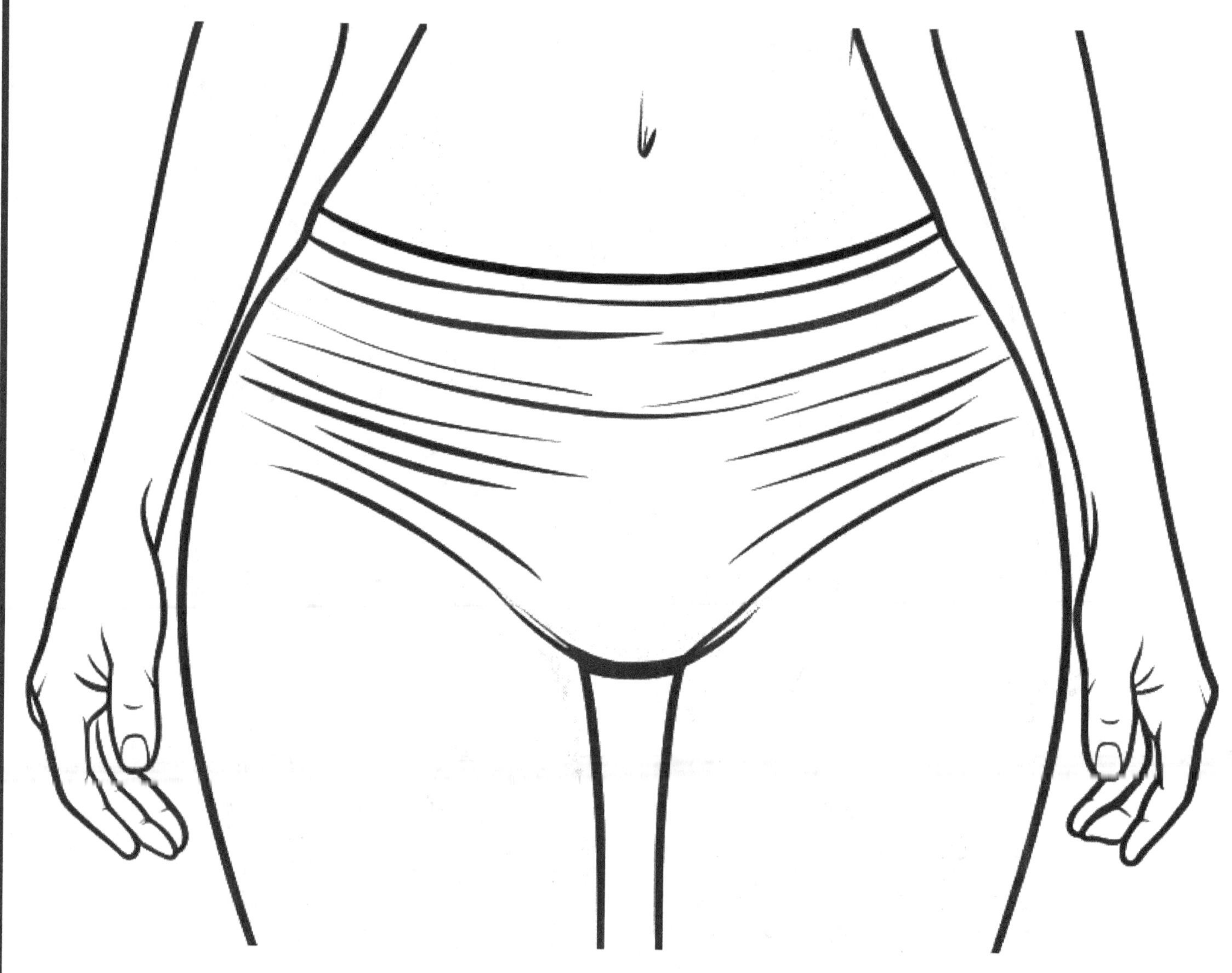

The female vulva and vagina

P p
is for Puss

A cat/ a thief

Q q
is for Quint

To wink, to bat the eyes

R r
is for Rock stone

A rock

R r
is for Rollin' Cyalf

A mythical paranormal creature created by storytellers to scare children; the subject of many aduppy story

R r
is for Reggae

A music genre that originated in Jamaica in the 1960's

S s
is for Spliff/skliff

A blunt, marihuana rolled in cigarette paper

S s
is for Soda

Any carbonated beverage

T t
is for Terbit

Term used to describe a muscular person "Tough like terbit"

U u
is for Ukubit

small

V v
is for Vanback

Tailgate of a pickup truck

W w
is for Woi-woi

A place far away

W w
is for Warboat

A person who fights often

X x
is for X-tray

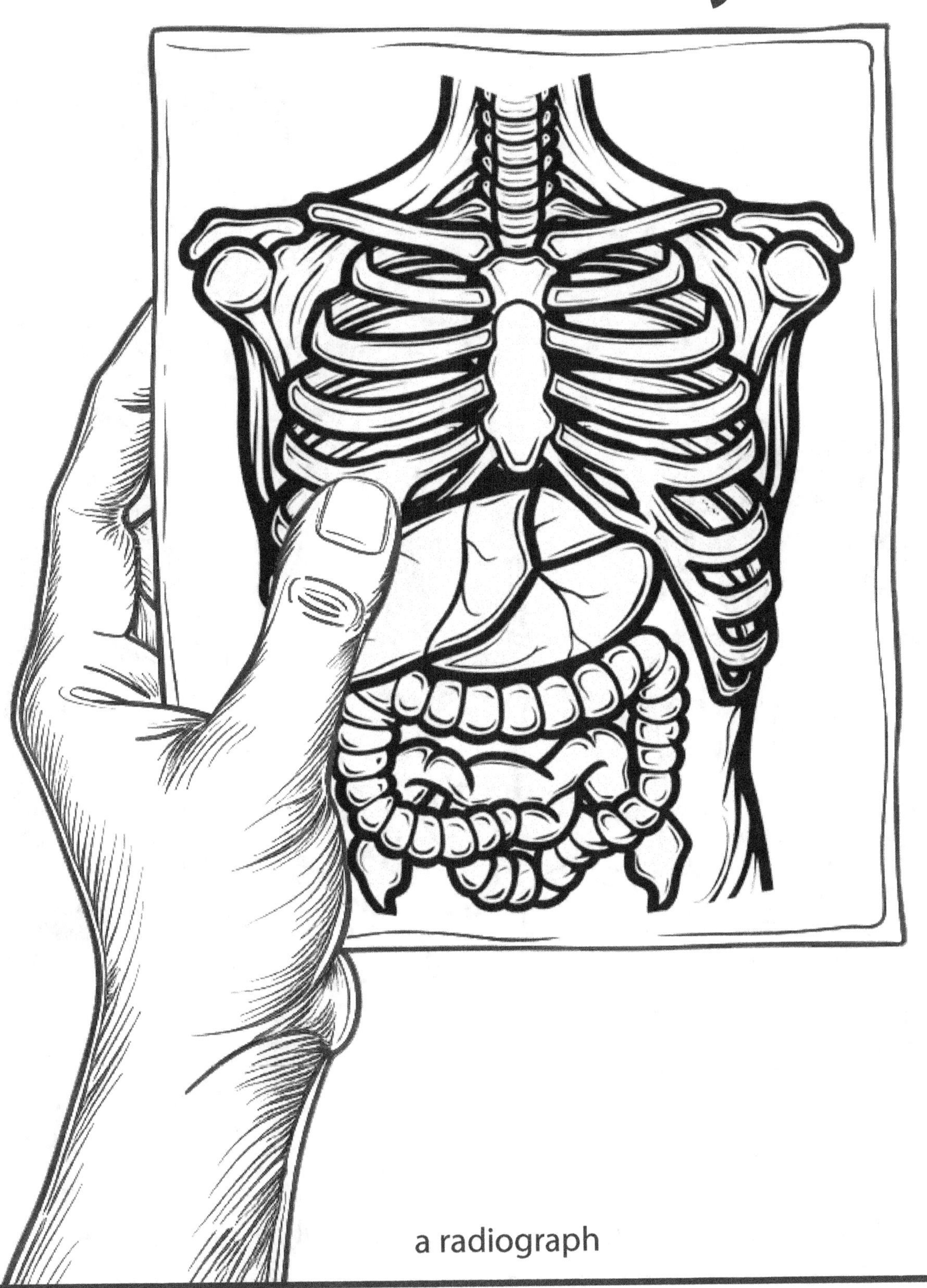

a radiograph

Y y
is for Yamhead

A gullible woman; usually one who believes what men tell them

Z z
is for Zutupek

An idiot

THANK YOU!

THANK YOU FOR PURCHASING

**A BLOODCLAAT COLORING BOOK:
AN ALPHABET COLORING BOOK INSPIRED BY EVERYDAY LIFE
ON THE MINI-CONTINENT OF JAMAICA"!**

WE APPRECIATE YOUR SUPPORT AND HOPE YOU ENJOY THIS UNIQUE COLORING
EXPERIENCE. EACH PAGE HAS BEEN DESIGNED TO BRING THE VIBRANT CULTURE
AND EVERYDAY LIFE OF JAMAICA TO YOU.

HAVE FUN EXPLORING THE ALPHABET THROUGH THE COLORFUL LENS
OF JAMAICAN LIFE!

IF YOU HAVE ANY QUESTIONS OR FEEDBACK, FEEL FREE TO CONTACT US

HAPPY COLORING!